Courage Is Contagious

Courage Is Contagious

• • •

And Other Reasons to Be Grateful for Michelle Obama

EDITED BY NICK HARAMIS

ILLUSTRATIONS BY JOANA AVILLEZ

NEW YORK

Published in the United States by Lenny, an imprint of Random House,
a division of Penguin Random House LLC, New York.

LENNY and colophon are trademarks of Penguin Random House LLC.

Hardback ISBN 978-0-399-59261-4
Ebook ISBN 978-0-399-59262-1

Printed in the United States of America on acid-free paper

randomhousebooks.com

2 4 6 8 10 9 7 5 3 1

First Edition

Book design by Susan Turner

Contents

• • •

Lena Dunham

Dear Reader,

It seemed like a no-brainer when, in the fall of 2016, *T, The New York Times Style Magazine* published a series of essays in appreciation of Michelle Obama. Saying goodbye to her was not just a duty but a celebration (albeit a bittersweet one, leaning more on the bitter than the sweet when we understood what was to come). Brilliant, kind, and irksomely stylish, she is beloved by anyone you would ever want to share a meal or a taxi with. Her influence on America—the way she injected the White House with a sense of class, ease, and definitive purpose (and not, refreshingly, any distracting controversy)—was obvious. But what was revealed in the writings of Chimamanda Ngozi Adichie, Rashida Jones, Jon Meacham, and Gloria Steinem was that Mrs. Obama had not simply gifted us with eight great years alongside her husband; she had also fully and completely rejiggered our notion of what a first lady could and should be. In the words of Adasendis De La Cruz, a very special ninth grader featured in this book: "I only care what certain people say, among them Michelle Obama."

But despite this mastery over both our moral and fan-girl selves, Michelle Obama was not born from whole cloth. She fought beside her husband as he made his way to the White House: against racist attacks, against the mainstreaming of their identities, and against her own reservations about being a political wife. But, forged in the fire, she emerged the most resilient and beloved first lady we have yet to know. She remodeled the job, and gave us a new sense of resolve.

Modern first ladies have been held to near-impossible standards of behavior, almost Victorian in the rigors of expectation. Their husbands become their mirrors, their albatrosses, and their legacies. Historically, style has been frowned upon—even if Lady Bird Johnson and Jackie Kennedy managed to slide some in—as were personal revelations (one of the reasons Betty Ford is so quietly remarkable). These women tried so hard to dress in ways that would invite neither approval nor scorn that they disappeared into a sea of beige organza. In effect, they were rendered human tea sets. Their intellect and opinions were used in service of their husbands' goals, and in cases of noncompliance (see: Hillary Clinton, Eleanor Roosevelt) the gavel was swift, merciless, and looksist. It ain't a job for the faint of heart, even if you do get to hang a painting of yourself in the White House.

Michelle Obama ignored many of these reductive constraints by being brazenly herself, by leaning even harder into what makes her so unique. She started out, of course, as a symbol, which Chimamanda Ngozi Adichie suggests when she writes, "All over America, black women were still, their eyes watching a form of God, because she represented their image writ large in the world." And yet she became so much more than simply the page of an illuminated manuscript. Using her Let Girls Learn initiative, Mrs. Obama made sure this country's young female population saw her (a lot of her) on the national stage (or on *Sesame Street*) and insisted that they had worth beyond what they meant to their fathers, brothers, and boyfriends. She became a champion for American fashion designers, making clothing easy and effortless and—perish the thought—fun. She invited self-expression into what had once been (and is alas again) the whitest place on earth. She mom-danced with Jimmy Fallon, she hugged children who saw what was coming in their political future, and she left us with this measured but potent call to arms: "When they go low, we go high."

I've had the good fortune to meet Mrs. Obama several times. The first words out of my mouth were, I'm sorry to say, "You're the most amazing person on earth, like way better than my mom even." I followed up that gem with, "I think I have that dress. Is it Band of Outsiders?" She thanked me for the way I modeled my womanhood for her girls, even if my show was a little "risqué" for the Obamas themselves (a brag I'll never get sick of bragging). She hugged me as if she wasn't forced into the arms of strangers hundreds of times a day. She told me I had something important to say. Even as a thirty-year-old ensconced in my career, I needed to hear that. Every woman does.

The second time we met was at a panel for Let Girls Learn. If you think you are going to say anything worthwhile on a panel with Michelle Obama then you are a delusional sociopath, so I simply soaked in what she had to offer about women, education, and the lack of opportunity that ferments when one is denied the other. Onstage, she told the audience that she often has to avoid "popping off" on Twitter, angry as she is at the state of the world. "Barack stops me."

"How do *I* avoid it?" I asked.

"You can do whatever you want." Again, I needed to hear those words.

When my Lenny co-founder, Jenni Konner, and I were presented with the opportunity to make *Courage Is Contagious* a book in our imprint, we jumped at the idea. This is the book I dreamed would be in my holiday stocking as a teen. It's the book that Jenni wants her daughter and her daughter's friends to return to again and again. It's the meditation we need in the hard times to come, a genuine and multifaceted appreciation of a genuinely multifaceted woman. We hope that by contemplating what Michelle gave us, some of her strength, her moral fortitude, and her powerful ability to override bullshit might rub off on us. Even just a little.

With love,
Lena

Nick Haramis

"Twenty minutes," they said. The summer of 2016 was coming to an end, and the Obamas were entering the homestretch of their second term in the White House. I'd asked Michelle Obama, through her communications director, to carve out five hours in her schedule to sit for the portrait that would eventually appear on the cover of *T, The New York Times Style Magazine,* where I was an editor. Normally I'd try for seven, but Mrs. Obama was, I'd assumed, a busy lady—little did I know at the time how true that was—so I suggested we cap the photo shoot at five hours. "We can give you twenty minutes." I responded with the haggling skills of a seasoned negotiator: "Okay, sounds perfect! Thank you so much!"

Introduction

I went to Washington the night before the shoot with the photographer, Collier Schorr, and the magazine's creative director, Patrick Li. I packed only a cashmere sweater and chinos—both new, both black, because the occasion seemed to demand reverence.

That morning, we arrived early at the South Lawn of the White House with instructions to enter a gate next to a set of pillars and an American flag. (If you should find yourself in this position, ask more questions.) Each time we approached a uniformed guard—with the rather preposterous assertion that we were "here to see Michelle"—we were directed toward a line of fanny-packed Germans waiting for their tour.

Eventually we made our way to the right gate, through a metal detector, and onto the South Lawn. The shoot was scheduled to happen in the Diplomatic Reception Room, one of three oval rooms in the building. It had four doors flanked by steely-eyed men with broad shoulders. (Days later, I would continue to worry that they were coming after me for the stack of paper hand towels I'd taken from the restroom.) A carpet in shades of blue and soft gold covered the floor, and the walls were papered with sweeping landscapes that had been handpicked by Jacqueline Kennedy.

When the middle of the room was cleared of furniture and the photographer's lights were mounted, the three of us were advised to stand on—and stay on—small bits of black tape placed on the floor across from the fireplace. I was sweaty, and not in a glowing way. And then Mrs. Obama showed up. I finally understood what it must have been like for all those stark-raving-mad teenage girls when the Beatles first landed in America. I wanted to hug her. I wanted to thank her. I wanted to shake her so that she understood the magnitude of her stronghold on America's collective heart. I also wanted a toilet, because I was convinced I was going to puke.

And yet, everything else disappeared the moment she introduced herself to us, and thanked us for coming. There was nothing scripted about the exchange; nothing to suggest pageantry. This was one of Mrs. Obama's last cover shoots as the First Lady of the United States of America, and you could tell just by looking at her. Gone was the stately hairstyle, replaced instead by straightened locks that pooled on her shoulders. Instead of a power suit, she wore a sheer silk top with silver statement earrings.

I'd never seen the first lady look like this. I'd never seen *any* first lady look like this. When she asked us to play Beyoncé on the stereo, and started dancing, her lips pursed, to "Formation"—when we *all* began quietly dancing—I knew I was in the presence of greatness. Not only was Mrs. Obama within reach, physically, but she also felt within reach on a symbolic level. It's a thread woven through this book, the sense that we aren't just in awe of Mrs. Obama, but that we see the best parts of ourselves in her. She famously told the world that when they go low, we go high, and in doing so, she met us all in the middle.

The shoot was over in a flash, and Mrs. Obama was ushered into the room next to ours to do an on-camera interview, and then she was off to Los Angeles to film a segment of *Ellen* in which she and Ellen DeGeneres would rummage through the shelves of a CVS. When Mrs. Obama left, so did everyone, it seemed. I remember looking up at a painting of George Washington and saying to myself, "Twenty minutes."

The following week, now that we'd taken the photos, it was time to set up an interview with Mrs. Obama.

Introduction

Through her communications director, and again with the haggling skills of a seasoned negotiator, I suggested we set aside an hour or two on the phone. The reply: "We're happy to answer some questions via email." This time, though, I didn't respond with, "Okay, sounds perfect! Thank you so much!" The email option, which made sense given Mrs. Obama's insane schedule, felt like a disservice to a woman who had devoted her life to serving others.

As I struggled to figure out a solution, I was reminded of an exchange I'd had in April 2009, three months into Barack Obama's presidency, with Kara Walker, the legendary black female artist whose paintings and black cut-paper silhouettes have long examined issues of race and gender, both historically and today. We were at an art party in downtown New York, and we had been drinking—I had, at least. Kara was filling me in on the details of a recurring dream she'd been having about Mrs. Obama. I asked her to write about it for me, which she did, nearly a decade ago, and which I will now share with you here:

> Last year, I met Michelle Obama in that brief, scintillating, oblique way of patrons and supporters. We shook hands, and I nuzzled in next

to her for a quick snapshot—several others were there, vying to be a part of the picture. I look smug, my hand cinched around her waist like a fresh suitor. Holding my champagne and leaning my head an inch away from hers, we are the same height, or maybe she is taller. I position myself as girlfriend, sister, fond acquaintance. I am hoping that she will realize how good I am to know. I make a lame joke. She responds with a knowing look that, I think, means she understands that I am an artist of some repute who could provide the White House with some art—that I could make it "clean." I even seem to believe this, my hand gripping the future first lady's waist. Lord.

Cut to two days later. I am in bed, and in the deepest part of the night my daughter stumbles into my room like a puppy, all gangly and grown outwardly. But a baby, still. It is dark and she is still sleeping. Is she frightened? Lonesome? Maybe both. I wake enough to turn down the corner of the duvet, and she slips into the spot beside me. I still sleep on the left—I like to drive.

I immediately reenter deep sleep, and this is what I dream: Michelle Obama turns the corner into my room, enters. She gently lifts the duvet up over my shoulders, smoothes it down, tucks down the edges a bit. I am enveloped in an aura of peacefulness and rest like I have not felt in years.

The next morning, I am embarrassed at having had a "mom dream," but find myself telling it anyway, hoping that some kind soul will share my comfort at having a black mother—I mean being a black mother—both. In my studio, I find myself staring into the sun and worrying that the "Black Maternal" is really not a new presence at all in seats of white power, or even the popular American mainstream. The last thing I want Michelle Obama to be is "America's Mom" for fear that ancient archetypes from Mammy through Lena Younger will predominate her characterization. But this seems impossible; this woman is actually very good at being herself. She's not a passive-aggressive construction or some pitifully noble bronze. She's way too smart and sexy for my narrow anxiety. Maybe I am just jealous, and I don't want to share her with anyone.

A few days later, I have a second dream. The circumstance surrounding this dream was the election of Barack Obama. I am walking down a red-carpeted White House staircase slightly behind Michelle, who has both adopted me and hired me as her personal assistant. I have a clipboard clasped to my chest and am eagerly awaiting her instruction as we head out to a waiting limo. Oh, my God, I really am regressing. The same warm feeling is there, of being the good daughter, the black girl who is real and here and loved—but this time, I am alert and eager. The dream has the feeling that I am putting my anxieties behind me in order to move forward with the work at hand.

Very good at being herself. Way too smart. Sexy. Each of us knew who Mrs. Obama was from the moment we were introduced to her. She hasn't changed. What she changed was us, encouraging us to lead better lives and teaching us to be better people through her example.

And so, I approached four writers from very different worlds—Chimamanda Ngozi Adichie, Rashida Jones, Jon Meacham, and Gloria Steinem—to contribute to the magazine by picking up where Kara left off almost eight years earlier, and to attempt the impossible: to put into succinct words the impact that Mrs. Obama has had on them.

Introduction

With this book, we opened up the challenge to a diverse group of artists and thinkers—from the president of Planned Parenthood to a Golden Globe–winning actress to two very special ninth-graders—with one simple question: "Tell us why you're grateful for Michelle."

Courage Is Contagious

Alice Waters

CHEF, AUTHOR, FOOD ACTIVIST

When I was a child, my parents planted a victory garden in our New Jersey backyard. That garden was responsible for my fundamental taste memories: sun-warmed strawberries, beefsteak tomatoes straight off the vine, sweet corn on the cob. It allowed our family to eat well, of course, but it gave us so much more than that; the garden connected us with nature and the seasons, helped us understand where our food came from, let us work the land and provide for ourselves and others. My parents were inspired to build their own garden because of Eleanor Roosevelt, whose victory garden on the White House lawn led to the planting of 20 million other victory gardens all around the United States when so much of the country's food was needed for the war effort. I grew up knowing that *that* was the sort of power a garden at the White House could have.

At some point after I opened Chez Panisse and became involved in the food movement, I started writing letters—rather fruitlessly—to presidents and first ladies about the idea of replanting one. I plagued Bill and Hillary Clinton about a White House garden for years and was a little appeased when Hillary planted tomatoes in a small plot on the roof. But tomatoes relegated to a rooftop weren't the fullest realization of what I'd envisioned: a lush garden of vegetables and fruits and herbs, flourishing out on the White House lawn, a public testament to our country's agrarian roots and the profound, paramount importance of real food, even when it's not a wartime necessity.

When I first met Michelle Obama in Chicago, early in 2008, during Barack Obama's first presidential campaign, I seized the opportunity to tell her my idea for a White House kitchen garden. She listened seriously, thoughtful and present as she always is, and agreed that a garden would send an important message to the country about how we should feed ourselves and our children.*

* I believe she had already decided to plant a White House garden long before I spoke to her, but was too gracious to say as much.

Though I felt hopeful after talking to Michelle, I was resigned to the inevitable bureaucracy that can slow down the simplest White House initiative. But I had underestimated her singular resolve and strength. A mere two months after Barack Obama took his oath of office, she and twenty fifth-graders from the local public elementary school broke ground on a thousand-square-foot organic kitchen garden—right out on the South Lawn, where everyone could see it.

Those pictures of Michelle digging in the garden with the elementary school students inspired people around the globe, just as Eleanor Roosevelt's effort had spurred Americans to plant their own gardens during World War II. From the day she broke ground, Michelle Obama welcomed children into the construction and upkeep of the garden. She admitted she hadn't been a gardener herself, but saw the possibility of changing not only the way her own children ate, but the way *all* American children ate, and dived in headlong. She understood that children are brought into a new and healthy relationship to food when they experience the slow, patient joy of working the soil, planting a seedling in the dirt, watching it flower and fruit through the seasons, then harvesting and cooking it when it is at the peak of ripeness. When kids have that experience, eating real food is as simple as falling in love.

The garden was just the first step in her pioneering Let's Move initiative. With intelligence, warmth, and humor, she confronted eating habits that had strayed from real food and were supported by the food industry and unhealthy school lunches. In the meantime, her garden grew in size and scope and beauty. And what a joy it was to watch it evolve over the course of eight years. Fruit and vegetable varieties multiplied, crops emerged in the garden from all over the globe—heirloom tomatoes, tomatillos, amaranth, Tuscan kale, Thai basil, anise hyssop—and the children and Michelle Obama planted Thomas Jefferson's heritage varietals of lettuce from Monticello. She had beehives installed in the garden and the honey harvested was used for a homebrew of White House honey ale. Some of the food grown there was used to feed the First Family or served at state dinners and receptions, and great quantities of fruits and vegetables were donated to a Washington, D.C., program that cooks healthy meals for the homeless. The food from the garden became a metaphor for the values of the First Couple, from welcoming guests to helping neighbors in need.

Her vision extended well beyond the boundaries

of the White House plot. In her final year as first lady, she took a nationwide garden tour, visiting schools and community programs around the country, and helped expand the idea of what a garden could be: gardens in truck beds, on rooftops, and suspended in air; gardens that included teaching kitchens where children learned to cook the vegetables they had grown; gardens so fecund that students held regular farmers' markets to sell their produce. Without Michelle Obama, the vital dialogue, so long overdue, now taking place at the intersection of food, health, agriculture, and the environment, would not exist. Since I started writing those letters decades ago, I always thought I understood how powerful the symbolism of a White House garden could be. But Michelle Obama's White House garden was so much more important than I could have imagined: It was a living, growing representation of the bounty and generosity and diversity of the United States—and of her own large-hearted, far-seeing vision for the future of food in this country.

Chimamanda Ngozi Adichie

AUTHOR

She had rhythm, a flow and swerve, hands slicing air, body weight moving from foot to foot, a beautiful rhythm. In anything else but a black American body, it would have been contrived. The three-quarter sleeves of her teal dress announced its appropriateness, as did her matching brooch. But the cut of the dress scorned any "future first lady" stuffiness; it hung easy on her, as effortless as her animation. And a brooch, Old World–style accessory, yes, but hers was big and ebulliently shaped and perched center on her chest. Michelle Obama was speaking. It was the 2008 Democratic National Convention. My anxiety rose and swirled, watching and willing her to be as close to perfection as possible, not for me, because I was already a believer, but for the swaths of America that would rather she stumbled.

She first appeared in the public consciousness, all common sense and mordant humor, at ease in her skin. She had the air of a woman who could balance a checkbook, and who knew a good deal when she saw it, and who would tell off whomever needed telling off. She was tall and sure and stylish. She was reluctant to be first lady, and did not hide her reluctance beneath platitudes. She seemed not so much unique as true. She sharpened her husband's then-hazy form, made him solid, more than just a dream.

But she had to flatten herself to better fit the mold of first lady. At the law firm where they met before love felled them, she had been her husband's mentor; they seemed to be truly friends, partners, equals in a modern marriage in a new American century. Yet voters and observers, wide strips of America, wanted her to conform and defer, to cleanse her tongue of wit and barb. When she spoke of his bad morning-breath, a quirky and humanizing detail, she was accused of emasculating him.

Because she said what she thought, and because she smiled only when she felt like smiling, and not constantly and vacuously, America's cheapest caricature was cast on her: the Angry Black Woman.

Women, in general, are not permitted anger—but from black American women, there is an added expectation of interminable gratitude, the closer to groveling the better, as though their citizenship is a phenomenon that they cannot take for granted.

"I love this country," she said to applause. She needed to say it—her salve to the hostility of people who claimed she was unpatriotic because she had dared to suggest that, as an adult, she had not always been proud of her country.

Of course she loved her country. The story of her life as she told it was wholesomely American, drenched in nostalgia: a father who worked shifts and a mother who stayed home, an almost mythic account of self-reliance, of moderation, of working-class contentment. But she is also a descendant of slaves, those full human beings considered human fractions by the American state. And ambivalence should be her birthright. For me, a foreign-raised person who likes America, one of its greatest curiosities is this: that those who have the most reason for dissent are those least allowed dissent.

Michelle Obama was speaking. I felt protective of her because she was speaking to an America often too quick to read a black woman's confidence as arrogance, her straightforwardness as entitlement.

She was informal, colloquial, her sentences bookended by the word "see," a conversational fillip that also strangely felt like a mark of authenticity. She seemed genuine. She was genuine. All over America, black women were still, their eyes watching a form of God, because she represented their image writ large in the world.

Her speech was vibrant, a success. But there was, in her eyes and beneath her delivery and in her few small stumbles, a glimpse of something somber. A tight, dark ball of apprehension. As though she feared eight years of holding her breath, of living her life with a stone in her gut.

Eight years later, her blue dress was simpler but not as eager to be appropriate; its sheen, and her edgy hoop earrings, made clear that she was no longer auditioning.

Her daughters were grown. She had shielded them and celebrated them, and they appeared in public always picture perfect, as though their careful grooming was a kind of reproach. She had called herself Mom in Chief and, cloaked in that nonthreatening title, had done what she cared about.

She embraced veterans and military families, and became their listening advocate. She threw open the White House doors to people on the margins of America. She was working class, and she was Princeton, and so she could speak of opportunity as a tangible thing. Her program Reach Higher pushed high schoolers to go further, to want more. She jumped rope with children on the White House grounds as part of her initiative to combat childhood obesity. She grew a vegetable garden and campaigned for healthier food in schools. She reached across borders and cast her light on the education of girls all over the world. She danced on television shows. She hugged more people than any first lady ever has, and she made "first lady" mean a person warmly accessible, a person both normal and inspirational and a person many degrees of cool.

She had become an American style icon. Her dresses and workouts. Her carriage and curves. Toned arms and long slender fingers. Even her favored kitten heels, for women who cannot fathom wearing shoes in the halfway house between flats and high heels, have earned a certain respect because of her. No public figure better embodies that mantra of full female selfhood: Wear what you like.

It was the 2016 Democratic Convention. Michelle Obama was speaking. She said "black boy" and "slaves," words she would not have said eight years ago because eight years ago any concrete gesturing to blackness would have had real consequences.

She was relaxed, emotional, sentimental. Her uncertainties laid to rest. Her rhythm was subtler, because she no longer needed it as her armor, because she had conquered.

The insults, those barefaced and those adorned as jokes, the acidic scrutiny, the manufactured scandals, the base questioning of legitimacy, the tone of disrespect, so ubiquitous, so casual. She had faced them and sometimes she hurt and sometimes she blinked but throughout she remained herself.

Michelle Obama was speaking. I realized then that she hadn't been waiting to exhale these past eight years. She had been letting that breath out, in small movements, careful because she had to be, but exhaling still.

Janet Mock

AUTHOR, TRANSGENDER RIGHTS ACTIVIST,
TV PERSONALITY

As I waited in line for a bathroom outside the Vermeil Room of the White House, Jacqueline Kennedy, painted in a floor-length peach gown, looked down at me from the wall, and I wondered if the other trans, queer, and bi women in line with me felt as out of place as I did. We were from across the country and were considered the next generation of LGBTQ leaders, all under the age of thirty, by the Obama White House. Together with Michelle, we toured the East Wing, we listened to policy roundtables, and we ate barbecue with Vice President Joe Biden and Dr. Jill Biden.

Growing up in Hawaii, I'd never imagined that my writing as a trans woman of color would open doors for me in Washington. That I was waiting to use a ladies' powder room in the residence of America's black first family, who had invited me here, felt like make-believe. Just two weeks before, I'd been curled up next to my boyfriend on a well-worn love-seat in our 400-square-foot Manhattan apartment, watching Michelle Obama speak at the 2012 Democratic National Convention. She'd hypnotized me in HD, as I watched her vouch for her husband—like me, an African-American who called Hawaii home. She smiled, she quipped, she was sincere. Casting off the constraints of first lady–hood in the brightest of colors, she wore a sleeveless A-line dress made of shimmering silk jacquard and designed by Tracy Reese, a similarly hued African-American woman.

I noticed how much more comfortable Michelle was on that stage than she had been in 2008—speaking to the audience, to me, as if I were her most trusted friend. Now we knew her—as well as we could know one of the most visible black women in the world—and she seemed willing to hand over her most private, genuine self.

She told us how "worried" she was when we all first met in 2008. How fearful she had been about life at 1600 Pennsylvania Avenue, built by slaves, and its potential to isolate her from the people she and her husband had vowed to serve. But instead of being overwhelmed by her new life, she leaned into it and made the role of America's first lady all her own.

Over the years, I have cackled and cried as she rapped about college education; surprised Americans on a White House tour; promoted vegetables with her viral Vine, "Turnip for What?"; and danced with Virginia McLaurin, a 106-year-old woman who said of the occasion, "I thought I would never live to get in the White House. And I tell you, I am so happy. A black president! A black wife!"

Michelle spoke it plain. Her gift was her ability to address the truth of the matter, and I always believed her—probably because she was not a politician, because she was doing unpaid labor, because she was investing her talents in a country that had often made her feel as if she would never measure up, never truly belong simply because she was a black woman.

Her long, dark, strong arms seemed broad enough to hold all of her selves: the descendant of slaves, the girl raised on Chicago's historically black South Side, the daughter of a Chicago city pump operator with multiple sclerosis, the Princeton- and

Harvard-educated lawyer, the hospital executive, the self-proclaimed Mom in Chief who knew she needed her own mother to help raise her daughters under the glare of the spotlight.

Whereas her husband—the son of a Kenyan man and a white American woman, raised in Indonesia and Hawaii—seemed exotic and almost post-racial, Michelle was familiar. She was an American black girl from a black neighborhood raised by and around black people. And for eight years, whenever I saw her—tending to her vegetable garden, boarding Air Force One, or walking alongside her daughters on the South Lawn—I heard the black feminist and educator Anna Julia Cooper's words:

> Only the black woman can say "when and where I enter, in the quiet undisputed dignity of my womanhood, without violence and without suing or special patronage, then and there the whole Negro race enters with me."

On that DNC stage in 2012, Michelle reintroduced us to the man with whom she fell in love. Her bright smile perfectly punctuated her frequently Tweeted line, "We were so young, so in love, and so in debt."

She highlighted Barack's guiding principles and in turn gave us all a moral roadmap to follow. She discussed the "values and visions" to which we, as citizens, should all aspire. She talked about showing gratitude for everyone, "from the teachers who inspired us to the janitors who kept our school clean."

One particular moment from that speech has become my own guiding principle: "When you've worked hard, and done well, and walked through that doorway of opportunity, you do not slam it shut behind you. You reach back, and you give other folks the same chances that helped you succeed." This sentiment had brought me to the White House just weeks after her speech. With Michelle's invitation, she seemed to be saying that this house belonged to me; it belonged to *us*—each and every one of us in that line who had, like Michelle, been told we did not belong.

I left the White House that day feeling uplifted and affirmed. For the first time in my young life, I truly felt as if I *belonged,* and that I was part of something so much larger than myself. It seemed to me that it was my generation's duty to, in her words, help "build a country worthy of [our] boundless promise." In their eight years in the White House, the Obamas pushed its doors wide open. They welcomed both the American people and a diverse administration that reflected the entirety of our country. They ensured that we all knew that the White House was not merely a monument—it was the People's House.

Back in 2012, when I watched Michelle from my couch, I was a young woman just entering public life. Like Michelle, I aimed to be a woman who used her voice for good. But I was nervous to live visibly. Only a year before, I had stepped forward publicly for the first time and told my story of growing up a trans girl in Kalihi, a low-income neighborhood on the island of Oahu that struggled with under-resourced schools, drug and gang culture, and poverty.

I had just begun to share the story of graduating with a scholarship, becoming the first in my family to go to college, attending graduate school in New York City, and embarking on my career as an editor in mainstream magazine publishing.

Michelle reminded me that I did not find this success on my own. My achievements were mine— but there were unnamed thousands before me whose presence, work, and sacrifices had paved the way for me: Audre Lorde and Maya Angelou, who created blueprints for writing one's self into history;

Marsha P. Johnson, Miss Major Griffin-Gracy, and Sylvia Rivera, who created blueprints for trans liberation; Barbara Smith, Gloria Anzaldúa, and Angela Davis, who created blueprints for intersectional feminism. In my own way, I felt called to do similar work, and spent my time speaking truth to power in ways that would tell the story of my communities— trans women and queer people of color who have resisted in the shadows, struggling to find welcoming spaces at school, at work, and in the world. I have tried to create safe havens for people who were pushed out of intolerant homes and onto the streets, who were unable to find employment, make a living, access vital healthcare, or just be themselves without the threat of exile, harassment, and violence.

As a journalist and advocate, I will tether myself to those fighting for freedom, equity, and greater access. I have done my part by letting my personal experiences serve as the root of my public podium, taking the stage at the United Nations, lecturing in the hallowed halls of Harvard, and addressing the pink-flushed masses at the Women's March on Washington. I have produced projects such as the HBO documentary *The Trans List,* which gave transgender Americans an opportunity—for the first time on television or film—to speak uninterrupted about their life experiences for an entire hour. And I have written two memoirs—*Redefining Realness* (2014) and *Surpassing Certainty* (2017)—that have offered girls growing up like I did a mirror so that they could better see themselves and dream of greater possibilities.

Like so many of the people I work alongside, I grew up fearful that if I were truly myself, I would be met with closed doors. Michelle Obama guaranteed that the doors to the White House, and all that they implied, would remain open. She made it clear that when she, as a black woman, entered that historic space, she may have been the first to be let in, but that it was her duty to ensure that she would not be the last.

Jason Wu

FASHION DESIGNER

When I was first asked to dress Michelle Obama in the fall of 2008, I wasn't familiar with who she was. I've never been that well versed in politics, but I did some research and was so inspired by her beauty and strength that I agreed to make a few custom pieces. Those early pieces led to me submitting a sketch for what would eventually become her first inauguration gown.

It was the opportunity of a lifetime to be considered for a project like that, and even though I had such a small team (myself and two others), we put our hearts and souls into making the dress. We scrambled to get things done on time, and I still remember the many late nights of sewing and draping. I think my naïveté at the time actually helped as I relied only on instinct—I didn't think too much about what people would say or think. The one-shoulder dress she ended up wearing was the first thing I sketched, on the corner of a piece of scrap paper.

In the weeks leading up to the inauguration, I didn't tell anyone I had a gown in the running. Every designer under the sun—every designer except me, that is—was expected to do it. When the day finally came, I was at home in New York, watching the inauguration—and later the inaugural balls—with my husband and a few friends. I don't recall the last time we'd all tuned in to watch an inauguration. I had never seen people my age and in the fashion industry so engaged in the political process. When Michelle Obama walked out at the inaugural Neighborhood Ball, and I realized she was wearing my dress—well, I was very emotional. It's hard to describe, but in that moment the dress felt like it embodied the hopes and dreams of an entire nation.

As soon as Michelle emerged, my phone started ringing. First, it was CNN. And then *The New York Times*. When things calmed down, my PR director came over to discuss what to do in the morning. By six A.M., I was on *Good Morning America*.

Before that evening, my brand had been recognized within the industry—I was already in stores such as Bergdorf Goodman and Net-a-Porter—but that dress and Michelle Obama made the brand instantly international.

I finally met Michelle later that year when we donated the inauguration dress to the Smithsonian Museum. She'd invited me to Washington so that we could present it together. She had also invited a handful of students to sit in the audience, to hear my story and hers, creating an educational moment at an otherwise ceremonial event. This wouldn't be the last time she leveraged a situation to help young people, but I do think it was one of the first times in her career as the first lady that I saw her take the opportunity to discuss a sartorial choice and to make it so meaningful. This would also be the first of many appearances that she would use as a platform for promoting fashion as a legitimate business.

Before the event, we were alone together offstage, and she gave me a hug. It felt like we'd known each other for years. She has a comforting spirit about her, and she makes you feel included, listened to, and important. That's part of her strength and her legacy: As smart and inspirational as she is, she is also completely relatable.

And she's not afraid of fashion. She looked at it

as an opportunity to cast the industry in a whole new light. It was no longer just a thing of vanity; it was a legitimate career in a creative field that created jobs. Not since Jackie Kennedy have we seen a first lady use her wardrobe to quietly express what she stands for. She championed different kinds of talents as exemplified by her Reach Higher Fashion Education Workshop, for which she invited roughly 150 students to the White House for a series of workshops and panels led by designers such as Diane von Furstenberg, Prabal Gurung, and myself.

Over the years, her choices became bolder. At first, her thing was niche designers. And then she became known for her sleeveless dresses, a daring choice in Washington, which is still very conservative—especially for a woman in politics. But she didn't conform to the boys' club expectations. Instead, she empowered women to embrace their femininity, insisting to them, by her example, that it's not a sign of weakness, but a sign of strength. She wore plunging necklines and bustier dresses, and yet, as different as she was from her predecessors, nothing she wore ever felt out of place.

After the inauguration, our relationship changed. I felt like I understood her. I knew what she wanted. We'd built a trust, and I have been designing clothes for her ever since. I suppose it's only fitting that my experience dressing the First Lady of the United States of America should end the way it began: with a surprise. I didn't expect her to wear a dress of mine to the farewell address. I'd made it months earlier as part of her wardrobe and had sort of forgotten about it. I wasn't actually watching TV that night, but someone called and told me to turn on CNN. It was yet another awe-inspiring moment for me, an immigrant whose dream was to come to America and be able to pursue a career in fashion. She'd taken my breath away exactly eight years earlier, and on the night that she said goodbye as the first lady, Michelle Obama did it again.

Cecile Richards

PRESIDENT OF PLANNED PARENTHOOD

No president in recent memory has done more for women than Barack Obama. But it wasn't just his policies that sent a message—it was his marriage to a brilliant woman every bit his equal, and the two fabulous daughters they've raised together. He wasn't afraid of strong women; he surrounded himself with them. It's impossible to overestimate the impact of having a president who values, understands, and supports women. A president who reveres his wife, not by placing her on a pedestal but by seeing her as a complex human being. A president and first lady who are deeply committed to building a future where his daughters, and all our daughters, have the respect and opportunities they deserve.

A graduate of Princeton and Harvard by way of

Chicago public schools, Michelle Obama was raised by parents who taught her to work hard and give back to her community. Had her life's path taken a different turn, it's not hard to imagine Michelle Obama the lawyer taking on issues of social justice, Michelle Obama the organizer, or even Michelle Obama the public servant running for office. Instead, she became Michelle Obama, our first lady. Like Eleanor Roosevelt and Hillary Clinton before her, she defied expectation and convention, carving out her role on her own terms. She championed women's empowerment both through the programs she helped create and by staying true to herself.

The first lady can transcend politics and stand for principles. Michelle Obama did this over and over again, staying above the back-and-forth of Beltway bickering while making her position perfectly clear. Like millions of Americans, Michelle Obama stands with Planned Parenthood. But more than that, she lives and breathes our values every day. She's smart, fiercely independent, and determined to chase her dreams. She worked hard to pursue opportunities in her own life, then reached back to hold the door open for all the women who would come after. She believes, as we do, that no matter where you come from, what you look like, or who you are, you deserve the freedom and ability to live your best life. She embodies the warmth and compassion Planned Parenthood extends to the 2.5 million people who count on us for healthcare each year.

I'll never forget when Michelle Obama spoke about the tapes that had come out featuring then–presidential candidate Donald Trump bragging about sexual assault. I was on the road in North Carolina and Florida. Her speech played and replayed all day on cab radios and airport TVs. Women stopped to watch with tears in their eyes. She captured what was on our minds and in our hearts. "I can't stop thinking about this," she said. "It has shaken me to my core." When she reminded us that it is not normal for a candidate—or anyone, for that matter—to laugh and brag about sexual assault, it felt like all of America let out a breath for the first time in a week.

She spoke for millions of us that day, not in political terms, but in personal terms—something she did again and again as first lady. Many of the issues she confronted—issues of race, gender, and the struggle for equality and opportunity—were emotional issues, and she never shied away from that. When we grieved a tragedy like the kidnapping of innocent girls by Boko Haram, when we celebrated a historic first like Hillary Clinton's nomination for the presidency, when our country stumbled on the long road to progress and seemed to slip backward on an issue like voting rights, we looked to her to put into words what we struggled to say. She was the voice of our better angels—a role she never asked for, but one she stepped into with grace and humility.

The early-twentieth-century activist and writer Emma Goldman espoused the idea that if she couldn't dance to it, it wasn't her revolution. During Michelle Obama's eight years in the White House, she danced to Beyoncé, broke a sweat in the gym, snapped along with the cast of *Hamilton,* encouraged young women to reach higher, called on our country and the world to "Let Girls Learn," raised her daughters to dream big, spoke truth to power, supported veterans and military families, and lovingly made fun of her husband. Watching the faces of the tour guests she surprised, it was clear: Having a first lady as kind, joyful, and down-to-earth as Michelle Obama was the revolution.

Our country didn't always do right by her, though. More than once, she became a proxy for the treatment of women in America. She drew ire from the same people who have always been threatened by a purposeful, empowered woman, and was often held to impossible standards of perfection. It isn't easy to go high when they go low, yet she took the high road more times than anyone should have to. She confronted hate and vitriol with poise and honesty, and reminded us all that it was never about her—it was about deep-seated racism, sexism, and bias. It was about the naked hostility too many women, particularly women of color, face every single day. Those are the issues she was determined to address. At times, it would have been easier to lash out or retreat from the public eye. But she never did. She left the White House with her head held high.

Michelle Obama is one of a kind, a role model for women and girls everywhere, someone who has touched countless lives. And here's the beauty: She isn't done yet. I don't know what she'll take on next, but there is no doubt in my mind that she is only just beginning to make her mark on a world that is better for having her in it.

Adasendis De La Cruz

NINTH-GRADER

I'm in love with a sport most girls don't play. When I was younger, my father and I watched boxing matches on TV, and I decided to learn the sport. My mother was worried I would get hurt, but my dream of becoming a boxer stuck. After three years of boxing classes, though, she's seen how good I am and worries much less. Most people say that pretty girls shouldn't fight, but I don't care what most people say. I only care what certain people say, among them Michelle Obama, who taught me that it's not just okay—but right—to pursue your dreams. You'd never know the challenges she faced by looking at her. And she instilled in me a similar sense of poise and determination.

A few months ago, I interviewed for a spot in an organization that gives kids the opportunity to box at a real gym while also getting help with their home-work. I was nervous, and my teacher came with me. She told me to act professionally, and not to joke or dance or be silly—the way I act when I'm playing around with my friends. I sat up straight and made eye contact with the interviewer, who spent most of the time telling me how good the program was. He asked me if I wanted to be a member, and I said I'd have to check with my mom. (She wants me to be-come a lawyer because I'm good at arguing, or a model because I'm always wearing her heels.) But looking at all the people training in the gym, I knew what my goal was. The interview was a success. I'd be able to go to his gym and train on Saturdays—which meant that I'd be able to get more one-on-one attention from coaches and train with people who felt as passionate as I did about the sport. I was also excited to have a real ring to practice in, rather than have to push desks out of the way. When I left the interview, I called my mom right away to tell her the news. She was so excited she told the whole family.

For the first few weeks, I felt welcome there, and I met a lot of other kids who also love boxing. But later, there seemed to be some confusion. My teacher reluctantly pulled me out of class one morn-ing to tell me she had bad news: The man I interviewed with told her I could no longer come to the gym for free because he thought I didn't need the help. He mistook my professionalism and eloquence for privilege. Maybe I shouldn't have sat there with my back straight and my hands folded in my lap. Maybe I should have worn baggier clothes. Maybe I should have fed the stereotype.

I felt like my dreams had fallen apart. The man didn't know anything about me. He didn't know that I came from a poor neighborhood. He didn't know that I've been raised by a single mother, or that I'm trying as hard as possible to help her, doing the dishes, mopping the floor, cleaning up after the dog, picking up groceries and her medicine. My mother and my two brothers were shocked when I explained to them what happened, but they told me not to worry, that everything always works out in the end. Secretly, I wondered if there was something I'd done to deserve this. Maybe if I had acted more "'hood," more "ghetto," they might have been open to helping me. But I pride myself on being professional and mature. I learned my manners from my classmates, my teachers, and the First Lady of the United States of America—and didn't expect them to be held against me.

Michelle Obama taught me that young girls can

be both pretty and strong. I never got back into the program, but that hasn't stopped me from moving the desks out of the way and boxing with some of my female classmates. I'm determined to become a professional boxer, and now even my mom supports the idea. The first lady has raised two wonderful daughters the same way my mom raised me: not to give up. Things happen that are beyond our control, but we have a choice to give up or to keep fighting. Life is like a boxing match. It's not about how hard you hit. It's about how many times you can take a hit and get back up.

Issa Rae

ACTRESS, WRITER, DIRECTOR, PRODUCER

In 2012, I collaborated on a parody video of Michelle Obama to "expose" what was really going on in her head. It started with putting ourselves in her shoes, imagining all the racism and ignorance—general buffoonery—that she's had to endure, but that she's been unable to acknowledge because of her role. *What must she be thinking behind that poise? And what if she said it out loud?* Yakira Chambers, the actress who played her, delivered lines like, "If it was me up there, I would have called Romney out the moment he said 'poor' instead of 'low-income,' but it wasn't me up there. Although it could have been. 'Cuz, I mean, my approval rating is high as hell!" Of course, this wasn't the real Michelle. We were just projecting ourselves onto her, but that's what I loved about having a black woman in the White House: So many of us felt like we could walk in her shoes. We understood her position.

Yakira and I came up with the idea while sitting around talking about Michelle and how proud we were of her. The sketch was motivated by admiration, but I still worried she might be offended if she saw it. I sent the first version to my mom—for advice, I always go to her—with the note, "I don't want anybody to find any excuse to criticize her because of this." At first, my mom was like, "Shut up, I'm sure it's fine." But as soon as she'd watched it, she changed her mind: "Don't you dare put this out! Ever. In your life."

We were protective of our first black first lady. I remember watching Barack in the primaries, before he had been elected for his first term. I'd looked up who he was and who his family was, and thought, "*What?* He's married to a black woman? And not only a black woman, but a *dark-skinned* black woman!" And then I learned more about her background—how intelligent she is, how she had reservations about him running for president. I identified with her, beyond the color of her skin, by how real she seemed.

I wasn't surprised by how levelheaded she was,

but, also, I was completely surprised by how level-headed she was! Even though I knew how accomplished she was, how did she stay so cool in the spotlight? I'd read about Michelle's mother staying in the White House to take care of Sasha and Malia, making sure they stayed grounded and didn't get spoiled. I'd never heard anything like that coming from the White House before. But of course their grandmother would be there! That's such a black thing, to bring the whole family around. It felt like they weren't letting the presidency faze them. They made the White House suit their lives rather than change themselves. I was surprised and proud. They felt so familiar to me.

I went to the White House for the first time when I was invited to attend their last annual holiday party, thankfully having forgotten about that video we made years earlier. My mom was the first person I thought to invite. We got through the endless security, at which point it all dawned on me in such a real way: *Here I am. A black woman. In the White House. Invited there by a black president and his black wife.* And then Barack came out, hugged my mom, told me he watches my show, *Insecure,* and made the announcement that Michelle was sick. In my head, again, I was projecting: "Yeah, she's sick—sick of all this shit!" And even though I never met her that night, her presence was felt in the warmth and positive energy that presided over the party.

While so many people have applauded her poise, her sense of fashion, her class, and her demeanor, others have been quick to tear down her appearance and compare her to a primate, a racist trope with a deep past. She must have been aware of every slight, and yet she never seemed to notice. Part of me hurt for her. I might not have been able to put myself in her shoes for a parody video, but I certainly understand the type of hatred that she must have endured, and I was proud of how she rose above it.

Her essence has bolstered my own confidence. It has allowed me, and the character I've created on my TV show *Insecure,* to expand beyond the idea someone else has of how a young black woman should behave. I don't need to prove anything to anyone. I can just be.

Every time I'm asked how I'm going to address the current presidency on my show, I stop and think about the statement I'd like to make. But ultimately the show itself is the statement. Twenty years from now, when *Insecure* is ancient, I want it to be very clear that the show came out during the Obama era as a result of the Obamas. I think people are going to trace back the renaissance of black American art—whether it's a painting by Kerry James Marshall or an episode of *Atlanta*—to having had them in the White House. I don't know that it's direct, but I believe we'll be able to connect the dots down the line.

Charlamagne tha God

RADIO AND TV PERSONALITY, AUTHOR

I went to a club the night Barack Obama became America's forty-fourth president. I didn't know this wasn't normal behavior—it was the first time I'd ever voted, and I wasn't alone. The club was packed with ballot virgins. When he won, everybody hugged and dapped each other up, and the DJ played Jeezy's now-classic record "My President." The chorus goes, "My president is black, my Lambo's blue / And I be god-damned if my rims ain't too." Most of us didn't have a blue Lamborghini, but we all had a black president, and that was what mattered.

As happy as I was, I was still a little skeptical about Obama's blackness. He was half-and-half to me. His father was black, his mother was white—and since I'm a conspiracy theorist, I thought there was no way in hell they'd actually let a black man become president in this racist-ass country. He was definitely the *black-est* president we'd had to date, but that wasn't saying much. I needed proof that he wasn't a plant, a Manchurian candidate who projected symbols of change and hope, but who was just being propped up to make it easier for "them" to manipulate us.

But then he walked out on that stage with Michelle and their two daughters. Of course, I'd seen Michelle during the campaign. I knew she was black. But seeing her that night, as first lady, I saw just how black she is. She could have been my sister, my mother, or my aunt. She was regal. Despite all the abuse and slander she'd suffered for months on the campaign trail, there was something about how she carried herself that night that wasn't just black. It was unapologetically black. Beautifully black. Pink oil moisturizer black. *Ebony* magazine black.

My first daughter was born in 2008, five months before Michelle Obama became first lady. Today I've got two daughters, and I feel privileged as a parent that the only first lady they've known until recently has been Michelle Obama. As my eldest grew up, I didn't see many positive role models for young black girls in the mainstream media. On TV, she had *Basketball Wives,* who aren't even married to basketball players. She had *Real Housewives of Who Gives a Fuck*. The black women on TV were often fighting over no-good men, or getting drinks poured on them, or shaking their asses in music videos. Michelle Obama changed that.

She was as visible as anyone on TV, and she presented an entirely different model for black women. No matter what the setting, Michelle always acted with poise. We never saw her slip up. Not once. Thanks to her influence, black women I know, including my daughters, felt more empowered.

My older daughter was naturally curious about Michelle. She would always ask me questions about her: "What does she do as a first lady?" "What was her job before this?" "Where did she used to live?" "Where did she go to school?" When I took her to Harvard with me to sit in on one of my speaking engagements, she was excited because she knew that's where Michelle Obama had gone. And now, all she talks about is going to Harvard. I love explaining to her that Michelle went to Princeton first, and then Harvard Law, that she was a successful attorney and university dean before becoming first lady. When I tell her about Michelle's journey, I can see the world open up in her eyes. And like Michelle and my two daughters, that world is beautiful.

Gloria Steinem

AUTHOR, ACTIVIST

Michelle Obama came into my life in stages. I knew that, like her husband, she was a Harvard-educated lawyer, but that unlike him, she had grown up on the South Side of Chicago, with parents who had not gone to college. When Barack Obama was a summer associate at her Chicago law firm, they met because she was his mentor. After his successful campaign for the U.S. Senate, I noticed that she chose not to go to Washington. Instead, he commuted to their home in Chicago where Michelle had a big job as head of community affairs for a hospital.

But she really entered my imagination once she became first lady, a tall, strong, elegant, and seri-ously smart woman who happened to live in the White House. She managed to convey dignity and humor at the same time, to be a mother of two daughters and insist on regular family dinners, and to take on health issues and a national food industry addicted to unhealthy profits. She did this despite an undertow of bias in this country that subtly questioned everything she did. Was she too strong, physically and intellectually, to be a proper first lady?

After a decade under a public microscope, she has managed what no other first lady—and few people in any public position—have succeeded in doing: She has lived a public life without sacrificing her privacy and authenticity. She made her husband both more human and more effective as a president by being his interpreter and defender, but also someone we knew was capable of being his critic. Eventually, she spoke up about the pain of the racist assumptions directed at her, but she waited until her husband could no longer be politically punished for her honesty. And she has always been the best kind of mother, which means insisting that fathers be equal parents. All of this she has done with honesty, humor, and, most important, kindness.

Over the course of the Trump-Clinton presidential campaign, Michelle became one of the most effective public speakers of our time. That's serious. To be less serious, she has always been a woman who knows the difference between fashion (what outside forces tell you to wear) and style (the way you express a unique self). At one lunch in the White House for women who had been spokespeople and supporters in President Obama's second campaign, she invited local public school children to sing and perform. Those students, mostly African-American kids, were spirited, talented, and at ease in a White House that belongs to them as much as to anyone in this country, yet they wouldn't have been there without Michelle.

Though I'm old enough to remember Eleanor and Franklin D. Roosevelt in the White House— and all the couples and families since—I have never seen such balance and equal parenting, such love, respect, mutuality, and pleasure in each other's company. We will never have a democracy until we have democratic families and a society without the invented categories of both race and gender. Michelle Obama may have changed history in the most powerful way—by example.

Patton Oswalt

ACTOR, STAND-UP COMEDIAN

I've never met Michelle Obama, but my late wife, whose name was also Michelle, worked with her in Chicago doing community outreach for the homeless. I heard stories about working alongside this very calm, very driven, very inspiring woman. Watching Michelle Obama, my Michelle learned how to be a role model.

But what really blew her away was that Michelle Obama was able to keep a measure of humor and grace when anyone else might have flipped out and screamed, "Bullshit!" There were moments, she said, when Michelle Obama wanted to do just that, but instead made a choice as though to say, "No, let's try to do something positive here and make this work." It's okay to get discouraged or pissed-off, but when Michelle Obama feels the same frustration and rage and despair as the rest of us, she doesn't let herself off the hook with "I can't even." She follows it up with "I *can* even." Lots of people think Michelle Obama is unflappable, but that's not what my Michelle saw. Someone who is unflappable might decide to turn away or give up to avoid getting upset. But Michelle Obama engages and says, "Okay, how can we fix this?"—that's true caring.

I remember when she appeared on *Larry King Live,* during the campaign in 2008. At one of the debates, John McCain had famously referred to Barack Obama as "that one," and everyone was like, "Oh, my God, he's so racist." But to Larry King, Michelle Obama said, "No, he was trying to say which senator voted for an energy bill that helps big oil companies. And he said, 'That one.' We're now all calling him racist, while he's trying to push through a really bad economic plan. And *that's* what we should be focusing on." It was a grown-up moment.

During Michelle Obama's time in the White House, instead of continually reminding us of her own role as an historic first, she seemed very aware of whose shoulders she was standing on. People like Eleanor Roosevelt or Hillary Clinton, or even Dolly Madison, inspired her—women who decided to take what has been, historically, a ceremonial role, and turn it into an opportunity to do something good for other people. Like those women, she was devoted to service. She left it to other people to discuss her place in history.

Anna Wintour
VOGUE EDITOR IN CHIEF

President Obama captured Michelle's appeal and impact perfectly when he said, "I think people gravitate to her because they see themselves in her—a dedicated mom, a good friend, and someone who's not afraid to poke a little fun at herself from time to time." I would like to add to that list of qualities Mrs. Obama's talent for dressing impeccably and appropriately—and how she defied the narrow confines of how you have to look when your spouse attains the highest office in the land.

I make no apology for calling out our first lady's taste in fashion as one of her achievements. No other American in the public eye has done so much to raise awareness around the rest of the world of our country's designers and labels as the industry here became a global powerhouse. That has been the case whether she was wearing some of our greatest and most famous names (such as Ralph Lauren and Michael Kors) or the new generation starting to make its voice heard (Altuzarra, Jason Wu, or Rodarte, for instance)—or whether she was celebrating labels, such as Ann Taylor and J.Crew, that embraced the idea that fashion could and should be a democratic (with a small d) pursuit. Of course, she didn't exclusively wear American designs. While in the global spotlight, she understood that she could use her fashion choices to pay a great compliment to another country, such as wearing Alexander McQueen or Peter Pilotto in the United Kingdom, Gucci in Italy. She knew from the very beginning that how she put herself together could underscore the optimistic, progressive, and empowered role she took in her day-to-day life. Far too often there's a timidity, a nervousness, about dressing well among those in the political arena, and it's to be hoped that in the many ways Mrs. Obama will be remembered as a standard-bearer for change, her boldness and brilliance with fashion won't be forgotten.

I was at the White House in October 2014 when the president and first lady flung open the doors to the fashion community for a fashion education workshop, to let young people meet designers and understand how what they did could be meaningful to their own lives. Of course, as with so much of what the Obamas have done in office, the event galvanized an entire industry. That day I watched as Prabal Gurung cohosted a panel discussion while Zac Posen ran a workshop with a rapt group of participants. Later on there was a packed cocktail party, and one guest, witnessing person after person taking pictures with their cellphones, remarked to me that it was hard to imagine that happening in the White House. To my mind it was a good thing—and an indication that we had a president and a first lady who lived in the real world.

Rashida Jones

ACTRESS, WRITER, PRODUCER

The first time I met Michelle Obama was at the White House as part of a mentoring initiative, for which the first lady had brought together a dynamic group of women to speak to urban teenage girls about their career goals. Olympians, actresses, producers, writers, an astronaut, and an Air Force general gathered in the West Wing to greet Michelle before we headed out to various local schools. She was warm, gracious, and charming. She thanked us for coming, hugged everybody, and made us all feel like her friends. As first lady, she has ticked all the boxes: loving wife, protective mother, health and fitness advocate, garden enthusiast and, yes, style icon. These accomplishments have left traditionalists feeling satisfied.

But, as is always the way, her reputation as the perfect hostess invited criticism from progressives. Enter Michelle Obama, outspoken activist, a woman who isn't afraid to remind us she is a proud African-American woman, which is, in itself, revolutionary. A former lawyer who speaks out on behalf of gay rights and gun control, she delivered an unforgettable speech at the 2016 Democratic National Convention, shining a clear, bright light on our country's shameful history. Suddenly, the progressives were pleased and the traditionalists were confused. The media wants to pin her down—they've been trying since Barack Obama took office in 2009. But you simply can't.

Michelle Obama embodies the modern American woman, and I don't mean that in any platitudinous or vague way. Rarely can someone express their many identities at the same time while seeming authentic. My female friends and I often talk about feeling like we're "too much." We're complicated; we want to be so many things. I want to be a boss and also be vulnerable. I want to be outspoken and respected, but also sexy and beautiful.

All women struggle to reconcile the different people that we are at all times, to merge our conflicting desires, to represent ourselves honestly and feel good about the inherent contradictions. But Michelle manages to do this with poise, regardless of the scrutiny. That, to me, is the best thing for feminism. Her individual choices force us to accept that being a woman isn't just one thing. Or two things. Or three things. The position of first lady is, unfortunately, symbolic, and that makes it fair game for media analysis ad nauseam. But no think piece can fully encompass a real woman.

If feminism's goal is equal opportunity and choice, Michelle makes me feel like every choice is available. You can go to Princeton and Harvard, you can rap with Missy Elliott, you can be a mother and a lawyer and a powerful orator. You can champion the Lilly Ledbetter Fair Pay Act while also caring about fashion. You can dance with Ellen and also fearlessly remind people, on live television, of the reality of your position: "I wake up every morning in a house that was built by slaves. And I watch my daughters, two beautiful, intelligent, black young women, playing with their dogs on the White House lawn." You can be your husband's partner and supporter, and also use your cultural and political capital to campaign for Hillary Clinton, unflinchingly standing up to her "locker room talk"-ing bully of an opponent with the battle cry "enough is enough!"—

eloquently putting into words what a lot of people, myself included, had been feeling.

Michelle Obama will have her own legacy, separate from her husband's. And it will be that she was the first first lady to show women that they don't have to choose. That it's okay to be everything.

Jon Meacham
JOURNALIST, EDITOR

On a lovely early autumn day in her final October in the White House, Michelle Obama stepped out onto a sunny South Lawn and, in a way, bid farewell. The setting was her celebrated organic kitchen garden, but the subtext seemed to go far beyond any single initiative. "I have to tell you that being here with all of you, overlooking this beautiful garden—and it is beautiful—it's kind of an emotional moment," Mrs. Obama said at a ceremony to unveil a bigger, fortified version of the garden. "We're having a lot of these emotional moments because everything is the last. But this is particularly my baby, because this garden is where it all started. So we're really coming full circle back to the very beginning." She recalled conversations in 2008 about the role she might play in an

Obama presidency—and noted, tellingly, that the garden emerged after "Barack actually won," to which she added: "He won twice." The gathered guests happily applauded.

There, in a way, was the essential Michelle Obama, or at least the essential observable version of herself: speaking of broad public good (the garden, which was part of her campaign against childhood obesity) while revealing an arch sense of competitiveness. *My husband won; he won twice.* As their history-making time in the White House came to an end, I pondered the lessons of the Age of Obama. My own view was that both the president and the first lady conducted themselves splendidly in the White House, managing the most difficult of tasks with apparent ease: projecting a grace that masked the ambition and the drive that took them, at early ages, to the pinnacle of American life.

In this they kept faith with a tradition that, in our country, is as old as George Washington, who embodied the classical ideal of Cincinnatus, the reluctant leader summoned from his plow to lead the nation. President Obama got much of the public credit for handling his eight years coolly, but the first lady was a critical element of his success. She chose her shots carefully—not least in choosing to make the case against Donald Trump on the campaign trail in 2016—and left the country with a warm impression of an excellent mother, a steady spouse, and a sensible, devoted American.

Not everyone agrees, of course; not everyone ever does. The Obama skeptics and the Obama haters have from time to time questioned her patriotism, but this is the same country that managed, in some quarters, to hold Eleanor Roosevelt in contempt. The important thing is that Mrs. Obama, a clear-eyed lawyer, found a way to withstand the scrutiny of the spotlight. In point of fact, she did more than withstand it. To borrow a phrase from William Faulkner, she not only endured it; she prevailed over it.

How? By finding, or appearing to find, that most elusive of things in the modern world: balance. She was not Mrs. Roosevelt or Mrs. Carter or Mrs. Reagan or Mrs. Clinton, playing roles in affairs of state. Instead she did what the first African-American first lady arguably had to do to play a successful public role. In Voltaire's terms, she cultivated her own garden, never threatening and never intimidating her neighbors. Much more doubtless unfolded beneath the surface or behind closed doors; history will sort that out. For now, it is enough to say that she left the

White House a strong and popular figure with a lifetime of good will and great reservoirs of capital on which to draw as she and her husband write their next chapters.

Back in 2008, musing on the life she was about to enter, Mrs. Obama recalled doubts about her garden—a bit of projection, one suspects, for doubts about the entire presidential enterprise. "What if we planted this garden and nothing grew?" Mrs. Obama asked. "We didn't know about the soil, or the sunlight. And it's like, oh, my God, what if nothing grows? . . . It was like afterwards I remember telling Sam [Kass, the former White House senior advisor for nutrition], 'This better work, buddy. This better work.'" And so it did.

Laura Camacho

NINTH-GRADER

"You should never view your challenges as a disadvantage. Instead, it's important for you to understand that your experience facing and overcoming adversity is actually one of your biggest advantages."

— MICHELLE OBAMA

I'm from Red Hook, Brooklyn. In the summer of 2014, I started going to the Brooklyn Public Library with a day camp set up through my local community center. They took us there on Thursdays, but after the very first visit, I knew that wouldn't be enough for me. I started walking there every day, past my school, past the public housing buildings and bodegas and parks. I'd see lots of people on the streets and sidewalks, kids running through sprinklers. But I'd keep going until I got to the library. Once I started reading, I couldn't stop. I even read one book, *The Summer of Letting Go,* four times.

When I returned to school that fall, conversations in class were suddenly interesting to me. I had opinions about the school-to-prison pipeline, stop-and-frisk, and the dehumanization of and discrimination against minority groups. We related these topics to novels we read, like *Night, Animal Farm,* and *The Absolutely True Diary of a Part-Time Indian.* From the ideas in these books, and others, I began to see the challenges people faced in my own neighborhood.

Growing up, I never thought of my neighborhood as different than others. I felt lucky to have the community pool, the baseball diamonds, the running track. We have a pier with a view of the Statue of Liberty. By the time I turned four, I was allowed to walk to the store alone with my grandmother watching from a window on the first floor of my apartment building. I felt safe because I knew that everyone in the building and on my block was looking out for me.

Watching the news, though, you might think that Red Hook was defined by gang violence. But we're so much more than just one thing. We stick together. Everybody knows everybody. We have two parks that are always packed with kids. The smaller one, called Tea Park, is where I learned to climb monkey bars. It's where I went with my brother and father, where I ran track without shoes, and where I made my very first friends.

It's also where, at the age of seven, in the summer after first grade, I got my first lesson in injustice. I was there on the Fourth of July the year Barack Obama was elected, barbequing with my family and friends and playing tag. I was trying to escape "it" on the slide when my nephew said, "Look!" I watched the police approach my brother and his friend. I remember exactly what my brother was wearing that day—a white T-shirt, baggy jeans, and a pair of Nike Air Max sneakers in green, white, and black. The officers told them to stand up and then patted them down. At the time, I didn't know what was happening.

Only later did I realize that they had been stopped and frisked, and not because my brother had done anything wrong. Suddenly, what I'd been reading about in books and talking about in class hit home (even though, strangely enough, we never discussed what happened as a family).

Witnessing social injustice has helped me to realize the importance of education. It's also motivated me to look beyond stereotypes and accomplish amazing things in my life. Michelle Obama has inspired me to learn more about current events in the United States and in countries where women have even greater challenges than we do. I want to keep reading. I want to hear what other people think, and I want to share what I think.

As Michelle Obama has taught me, overcoming adversity allows me to see the world differently than someone who has had it easy. When I was younger, I didn't even realize that we lived across the street from one of the largest housing projects in New York. To me, they were, and still are, just houses. And now, when people look at Red Hook and see drugs, violence, and gangs, I see a community of people working together and helping each other.

There's a lot I want to do with my life. I want to teach. I want to write. I want to play basketball. I am the captain of the Pave Panthers, the women's basketball team at my school. I'm proud of that accomplishment, and proud to motivate other girls on the team to reach their goals.

Red Hook has been a wonderful place to grow up, and it's given me one of my biggest advantages in life by teaching me to overcome disadvantage. Michelle Obama has inspired me because she, too, was passionate about doing well in school. She, too, came from a modest neighborhood. She, too, worked hard with what she was given, and that turned out pretty well for her. Michelle Obama has shown me that even though I am just a girl in Red Hook, Brooklyn, I can do anything.

Gabourey Sidibe

ACTRESS, AUTHOR

My first visit to the White House, for the 2010 Correspondents' Dinner, wasn't the greatest. I made a joke that inspired some dude to write an article about how terrible I am. We had all laughed about it at the time, but cut to the following day: "Gabourey Sidibe is a piece of garbage." The article came out on my birthday. I was like, "Now I can never go back."

A few years passed. It was 2015, and I was thinking, "Not only am I never going to get to meet the first black president of America, but also the first *African-American* president." Like me, half of him is African, the other half American. Like me, he has a name that's really hard to pronounce. But somehow I got invited back.

When I arrived, it was all red carpets and politicians. I was meeting everybody and posing for pictures, and I was sweating because I was wearing a big black-and-gold ball gown. I'd put a lot of work into the outfit because I wanted to go super African-American. I'd even had my hair done in Senegalese twists. It was important for me to represent that part of myself, but also I was trying to survive while in heels and drenched. I was ready to die.

Then this woman tapped me on the shoulder, and she said, "You've been invited to a private reception with President Barack and First Lady Michelle Obama." I was like, "Uh, take me there immediately." We had to go through an additional metal detector, which was fine—I went to high school in New York City. I got through and they handed me a piece of paper with my name written on it. It was typed up and cut out, so clearly this was planned. It wasn't like, "I guess Precious is here, so we should include her." I was so confused by the piece of paper that I actually asked what to do with it: "Is this mine? Do I get to keep this?" And they were like, "No, when you get up to the Obamas, somebody will take it from you and announce you."

Before that happened I saw a bathroom, thankfully; at that point I was my own personal Atlantic

Ocean. There was another lady in there, standing at the mirror, wearing a sparkly red dress. She looked great and calm, and she didn't really notice me. But then I turned to her to say, "I'm going to meet the Obamas!" I'm sure she thought there was something wrong with me, like I was having a mental breakdown. The woman said to me, "It's okay, girl. You're going to be fine." She probably worked with them, or under Tina Tchen, and there she was, giving me a pep talk.

She left, and I patted my face some more and returned to the receiving line. Next to me, waiting to meet the Obamas, was a woman who was also my kind of African-American. Again, like a child, I screamed, "I'm going to see the Obamas!" And she was like, "Yeah, me too. We're both in the line for that." She probably assumed I was insane as well. But talking to her relaxed me. She was a fan, I guess, and was telling me that I was cool and important or whatever, which made me reconsider my right to be in the room. I thought to myself, "You're talented and you use your voice and you are impactful. But more than that, it's okay for you to be here. You did not win some contest. You didn't get through the door by selling Avon. You are here because you are one of them." The second I reconciled that in my brain, I stopped sweating. All of my nervousness went away, all of the butterflies shot out of me.

I handed my name to the person who was supposed to announce me, but before they could, Mr. Obama said, "I know who you are! You're the bomb, girl." He hugged me, and without really thinking, I said, "Shut up, Mr. President!" And then Mrs. Obama said, "You just told the president to shut up." And she chuckled, like, *You did it, girl. You really took a chance.* And then they held me, as if they were my aunt and uncle and we were at my graduation barbecue.

Michelle is so important to me, not just because we're both black—although there is a lot of black pride and #BlackGirlMagic in me. She's wonderful to me as a person, not just as a black person. The way she cares about others is nothing short of remarkable. Her Let's Move initiative, focused on educating schoolchildren about exercise and healthy eating habits, was done with so much love.

I was born in 1983 in Bed-Stuy, Brooklyn. The fathers of my friends were largely in prison or dead. I thought my only escape from that world was to play basketball, to rap, or to dance really well. Harvard, Stanford, Princeton—none of them were on the table, at least not for us. But what Michelle showed me was that you can go all the way to the White House, and that it has nothing to do with how fast you can run or how many bars you can drop. It has to do with your brain.

I might never get invited back to the White House, and I'm okay with that, because I will never forget being in that room with Michelle. There is an air about her, an aura. It's her humanity, and I'm reminded of it every day when I think about Michelle saying, "When they go low, we go high." It's the only thing dragging me through the current presidency, because what's happening now is really, really, really low. The names I'm called on social media, the number of people telling me to go back to Africa—it's really, really, really low. And it makes me want to go lower. I want to tell them that they are nothing, that they will always be nothing. But then I hear Auntie Michi in my ear, and she's right: There is a sense of strength that comes from going high. It's what I hold on to, and it's what I will keep holding on to.

Kate Millett

AUTHOR, ACTIVIST, EDUCATOR

The power of blackness, its beauty and magic, lives in Michelle Obama. Which is why it affects me in my gut to see such an iconic figure so susceptible, so vulnerable, to criticism and barbs and other petty attacks. She is human, of course, and yet better than that; that the monsters of this country could ever wound her is surprising.

The story of Michelle's public ascent is also the story of blackness in America, all the way back to Sojourner Truth, whom the former first lady memorialized with a bust in the U.S. Capitol back in 2009. After years of trying, the National Congress of Black Women succeeded in erecting a tribute to the early-nineteenth-century abolitionist and women's rights activist. During its unveiling, Michelle stood next to

Nancy Pelosi and said to the assembled crowd, "One could only imagine what Sojourner Truth, an outspoken, tell-it-like-it-is kind of woman . . . what she would have to say about this incredible gathering. We are all here because, as my husband says time and time again, we stand on the shoulders of giants like Sojourner Truth. And just as Susan B. Anthony, Elizabeth Cady Stanton, and Lucretia Mott would be pleased to know that we have a woman serving as the speaker of the House of Representatives, I hope that Sojourner Truth would be proud to see me, a descendant of slaves, serving as the First Lady of the United States of America."

I'm reminded of that speech every time I think about Donald Trump's defiant boast that, because of his fame, "They let you do it." In that one unapologetic outburst of misogyny, I saw the history of white male privilege flash before my eyes. How deeply each of his attacks on women must have cut Michelle, as they did so many of us. How hurt she must have felt about the vileness of his boasting.

To me, it's better that Michelle isn't interested in running for office. She's too good for it, and in truth, she can accomplish much more outside of it, such as continuing to travel the world, giving generously of her time on behalf of women who were trafficked and sold into slavery. There's so much to do, so much injustice to fight against, in and out of our country. How about she join the staff at Columbia University to create an agenda for education in prisons? Most prisons are hell on earth—noisy, full of gossip and small-mindedness, brutality and authoritarian oppression. Education is a corrective to this, and, as has been proved time and again outside the walls of a penitentiary, a source of healing and hope. It's an idea, albeit one among many.

I know I'm asking a lot, and what Michelle has already done is surely enough. But even though she's no longer in the White House, I keep coming back to her. I keep thinking about how hard she fought—about how hard it is to fight, from my own experience—and how much, now more than ever, the American people need her. How much, now more than ever, women need her. How much, now more than ever, I need her.

Tracee Ellis Ross

ACTRESS

I have been to the White House many times. I was there with Jimmy Carter, as a child—I have a signed picture of him from the visit. I was there again with George W. Bush, when my mother, Diana Ross, received the Kennedy Center Honors. The house felt entirely different after the Obamas moved in. They had clearly decided to make the White House feel like our house, or perhaps the decision was made simply by having them there. They passed the torch back to the American people, as if to tell us that this is our country and that we do have the power. They took their power and used it to empower others.

I first visited the Obama White House in 2011 for one of Michelle Obama's mentoring events timed to Women's History Month. There's a photograph of the two of us from that day. We're in profile, and we are talking with our hands. Her hand is down and my hand is up, and it looks like there's a bird between us. When I think back to that photo, it's clear to me that we were just beginning a conversation about being proud, powerful black women in this country, which continues to this day and stays alive whether we see each other or not.

To be in partnership with your husband and to also have your own life is not original, at least not in real life. Having that combination embodied in a figure as archetypal as the first lady has had a huge impact on our culture. She didn't shy away from being a loving wife. She didn't shy away from the importance of fashion to her role. But at the same time she was robustly herself.

Our show, *Black-ish,* is a family comedy, and what we're playing is an American family. We don't happen to be black. We *are* black. Mrs. Obama made room for my character, Rainbow Johnson. She validated a Rainbow Johnson for people who had never met a black woman with the revolutionary experience of being joyful. A black woman who is not only surviving, but thriving. A black woman who is actually in love with her husband—not an image we usually see in American pop culture. A black woman who can be goofy and sexy, who can be smart and empowered and soft and lovable and vulnerable. Eight years of watching Michelle Obama as a *person,* not just relegated to doing "woman things," provided an antidote to all the false representations of black women that have inundated us for centuries— images that don't represent the reality, or the humanity, of who we are as black people. Of who we are as people. And then to have her name prefaced by two things that are rarely associated with black women—"first" and "lady"—well, it shattered everything.

Part of what Mrs. Obama has encouraged in me is the strength within myself to be myself. It's not the White House that made her who she is. She *is* who she is, and it's something we were reminded of time and again during her final year there. She said in her speech at the 2016 Democratic National Convention, "I wake up every morning in a house built by slaves." She didn't deny the history of this country. Instead she acknowledged it, as if to emphasize how far we've come and how important it is for us to keep moving forward. In another speech, following the release of footage that captured Donald Trump talking about grabbing "pussy," she stood at the podium and said, with tears in her eyes, "I can't believe that I'm saying that a candidate for president of the United States has bragged about sexually assaulting women." She named what so many people would not name, what so many other women were shamed out of naming. To have the First Lady of the United States stand up and name what was happening for all of us put the shame back where it belonged.

Somehow, I think we saw her become more herself during her eight years in the White House. The more the wind whipped around her, the sturdier she became. The larger her platform, the deeper her roots stretched and the longer her branches reached. It wasn't exactly a blossoming, but a ripening.

Acknowledgments

I'd like to thank my former boss and forever mentor Deborah Needleman for trusting me with a Michelle Obama cover story when I was still one of her editors at *T, The New York Times Style Magazine*. Without the original essays we made together, this book would not exist. I would also like to thank another onetime *T* colleague, Whitney Vargas, for introducing me to the wonderful team at Penguin Random House.

To that end, I would like to thank my inspired and inspiring editor, Hilary Redmon, who came to me with the idea to put together this collection. I'm also grateful for my agent, David Kuhn, for his support and guidance—and killer negotiation skills. I owe a debt of gratitude to Jenni Konner and Lena Dunham, who, during a particularly frenzied time for me, calmed my nerves with an email that included both the word "aplomb" and the suggestion that we become friends.

I need to thank Kelsey Donahue and Caroline Adler Morales, from Michelle Obama's team, who helped me navigate the White House, literally and figuratively.

There's also Molly Turpin, William LoTurco, Joana Avillez, Kerry James Marshall, Minju Pak, the book's incredible contributors, my family, my friends, and my patient and all-around-perfect boyfriend. Thanks, Misha, for not dumping me when I was my most fully realized train wreck.

And, finally, of course, I need to thank Michelle. So thank you, Michelle. Thank you, thank you, thank you.

About the Editor

NICK HARAMIS is the editor in chief of *Interview,* an arts and culture magazine founded by Andy Warhol in the late 1960s. He lives in New York City, and hadn't really considered moving back to his Canadian hometown until around 12 P.M. Eastern Standard Time on January 20, 2017 . . . give or take.

Instagram: @nickkharamis